Looking & Longing

Looking & Longing

**A course
to rekindle
the spirit
of Advent**

DAVID ADAM

kevin
mayhew

First published in 2003 by

KEVIN MAYHEW LTD
Buxhall, Stowmarket, Suffolk, IP14 3BW
E-mail: info@kevinmayhewltd.com

KINGSGATE PUBLISHING INC
1000 Pannell Street, Suite G, Columbia, MO 65201
E-mail: sales@kingsgatepublishing.com

9 8 7 6 5 4 3 2 1 0

ISBN 184417 143 4
Catalogue No 1500634

Cover design by Angela Selfe
Edited by Katherine Laidler
Typesetting by Louise Selfe
Printed in Great Britain

Contents

Acknowledgements

The publishers are grateful to the following for permission to reproduce their copyright material:

SPCK for two prayers: 'Inner longings' from *Power Lines* by David Adam, published by Triangle/SPCK, 1992, and copyright © David Adam; and 'Come, my Lord' from *The Open Gate* by David Adam, published by Triangle/SPCK, 1994, and copyright © David Adam.

Church House Publishing for the prayer 'May the humility of the shepherds' from *The Promise of His Glory*, published by Church House Publishing, 1991, and copyright © The Archbishops' Council of the Church of England.

The prayer 'We pray you, Lord' by William Temple (d. 1944) is © copyright control.

Every effort has been made to trace the owners of copyright material and it is hoped that no copyright has been infringed. Pardon is sought and apology made if the contrary be the case and a correction will be made in any reprint of this book.

Introduction

Advent is an important season in the Church and it is being lost. Fewer and fewer Christians celebrate Advent because they have relegated its meaning to a far distant future. Advent not only means 'to come', it also means 'to arrive'. In reality Advent always is with us. Advent celebrates the eternal coming of our God to us and to the world. If we do not grasp the meaning of Advent, then we shall not really enter fully into the reality of Christmas. I was once asked when I thought the crucifixion began. I replied, 'When Adam and Eve disobeyed God in the Garden of Eden.' The first verbal record of God's coming is also in the creation story, which includes God seeking Adam and Eve after their disobedience. God calls to the couple, 'Where are you?' This is still the major question of Advent: where are you in relation to God's coming? I like the Wayside Pulpit notice that says, 'If you feel that God is far off, who do you think has moved?' Advent is not only God's coming to us, it is our coming to God. When we pray, 'Come, Lord, come among us', it is not so much we are asking God to descend from a height as we are opening our lives and hearts to the God who comes. The Advent experience should be one of the most important stages in our faith. If our God does not come, we can have no faith relationship with him.

If life is frustrating, if it feels like you are living in a wilderness, or are not at home in the present, if you long for something better, you wish a new day would dawn, if you feel a deep emptiness within, then the Advent time is already yours. God comes to you and is calling you. Will you respond and let him arrive in your life? All the great seasons of the Church, such as Advent, Christmas and Easter, are seasons of our lives and at the same time are eternal events. Advent is not just a time before Christmas; it is now, and yet in another way not yet: we have to allow our lives to experience this deep mystery. It is the same mystery that allows Jesus to be described as the Lamb that was slain before the foundation of the world.

What you look for in God's coming, what you long for, is actually happening if you have eyes to see and a heart that is aware. Advent calls for our attention and our awareness; it calls on us to be alert, to awake out of sleep. One of the aims of this book is to help us to open our blinded eyes and see, to open our ears to God's call and to open our hearts to his love. We shall use not only the four weeks of Advent but also the Christmas season and Epiphany to celebrate the coming and arrival of our God. To help us, we shall look at characters from the Old and New Testaments each week and see where we stand in relationship with them. The reason for continuing to Epiphany is that this festival celebrates God's coming to all the nations of the world. As Advent rejoices in the God who comes, Christmas and Epiphany show that we can come to God. The coming of lowly shepherds and non-Jewish seekers in the wise men tells us that all who will may come. God comes to you; become aware of this and come to God.

I want to use a method of approach to each week that I have called the X-Files. For this approach to be really successful, it would be better if every member of the group had a copy of this book. We cannot achieve much in an hour together unless we have done some work at home. Ideally you will work on a passage for a week before coming to a meeting; this way you will be enriched and be able to enrich others. The X-File approach works like this:

EXTRACT yourself from your busyness, learn to be open and still before God. Spend some time relaxing in the presence of him who comes. Let go of such a tight grip and let God have some control. There is no need for many words; be still and know. Invite God into the space that you make. You might like to say quietly, 'Maranatha. Come, Lord Jesus.' I have put an opening prayer and other suggestions at the beginning of each session to help you to open up and become more aware of the abiding presence of God.

EXCERPT from the Scriptures the passages to be read. To make this easier the excerpts have been printed in full in each chapter, though I do believe it is good to become familiar with your Bible and to know where the various books are in relationship to each other. Read the passage slowly and try to see it. If possible, bring a Bible with you as well as this book.

EXPAND the passage by bringing all your senses to bear upon it. Not only see what is going on, try to imagine you are there. Can you hear the sounds? Can you feel the objects around you? Can you taste or smell anything? Try to get a full picture of the situation. When I was acting in pantomime a friend who produced always said, 'Make it bigger, make it bigger'; you are asked to do this with the story you read. You might like to make a few notes of the event in question.

EXPERIENCE. Let your own life's experience enrich the scene before you. Have you been there? Do you know how it feels? Do you see yourself in the picture? Can the story be used as a mirror for events in your life? Very often the Bible stories we hear touch on our lives and our own personal situation. Let the Word of God speak to you and your experience.

EXPRESS to others where you stand. This is not for discussion or debate. Each person can say how they feel like Adam, or Mary the sinner, or the wise men. Much of the time we may really feel like Abram, 'not knowing where he was going'. This is to help us to see and say at the moment, 'Here I stand.' This can be very revealing but leave comments until later.

EXPOUND. This is group discussion time, but it should not be too long. The leader of the group should regulate this time and not let it exceed 15-20 minutes. Good time-keeping is important. I am always worried about groups that talk a lot about God and not much to him! Too many people have theories about God, but lack a personal relationship with him. However, discussion time is a time for giving attention to each other. I believe that if we are unable to give our attention to another, we will be unable to give attention to the great other who is God.

Group time tells us much about our willingness to be open and alert to others. This is a time to discuss what action or what vision follows our readings. What we truly learn and experience should change our lives. I have provided some thoughts for the group discussion time.

EXULT. Give thanks to God for new insight. Give praise to the God who comes to you now. Relevant music and prayers should be included here; some are suggested but you should be able to add others.

EXPECT. Go out and look for the change this new relationship and knowledge have made to your life. Know that the God you talk about is with you now. Take moments off to rejoice in his presence and his love. It is too easy to say, 'He will come again', and imply that he is somewhere else at the moment. It is too easy to live as people without God, and that is to be faithless people. 'The Lord is here' is a reality. Expect your awareness of this truth to grow.

There is no need to go through all the stages of the X-Files, but they will give you a good structure to build on and help you to move from one kind of experience to another.

Because our experience is more than we read and hear, more than mere words, I hope a meeting of any group will be enriched by the use of visual aids and music. It is a good idea, while a group is gathering, to have some quiet music. This does mean that it would be beneficial for a CD player or a cassette player to be made available each week. Once all are gathered, a visual focus, such as a picture or a candle, may be used for the early stage of prayer. As it is Advent it is good to have an Advent wreath.

To make an Advent wreath make a circle of greenery (this reminds us we are dealing with eternal events). Add four candles (some people like to use purple candles to say it is Advent). In the centre of the circle add one larger candle to represent Christ's arrival,

God-with-us. Advent is at the darkest time of the year, so it is good to bring a little light to it. The first week we will light one candle, the second two, and by Christmas we will light all five. We will continue to light them each week until the last week. We can either let the ones that have burnt out be left out or replace them with others. To make a simple wreath, I have used small tea-lights on a plate with four around the outside and one in the middle and replace any that burn out. With this simple wreath you can add a little greenery if you so wish.

Another good idea is to have or make some crib figures – Mary, Joseph, Jesus as a baby, shepherds and wise men (we have often added a wise woman too!). In Advent, Joseph and Mary can travel from house to house, seeking room and welcome. Each house they enter can say a prayer of welcome and light a light for the coming of the promised One. This is very useful teaching if there are children in the group or at the home of a member of the group. I have always found it surprising just how many young children would like to say a prayer with Joseph and Mary for the baby Jesus. It is worth buying a cheap crib set for this occasion. Maybe you will begin a tradition in your area. Sometimes, I have asked others outside the group if they would like to put up Joseph and Mary for the night. I have found this a good method of outreach.

The group may like to bring cuttings from magazines illustrating the meaning of a session. These could be put into a scrapbook or put on display in church. To aid the memory, the picture will need some captions. Or the group may like to make an Advent calendar, not of dates but of events that lead to the coming of Christ. It may be possible for a Christmas card to be designed, perhaps a little competition, and then displayed in church.

I have assumed that if it is a group meeting, there will be a leader each week to help the group to follow the pattern and to encourage all to partake fully. If possible, it is good to have a different leader each week. For the leader to be effective they must have worked over the session at home, preferably two or three times before the meeting. It may be a help to have a page entitled 'X-Files' as below:

EXTRACT	Time of candle lighting, quiet music and stillness. (About 10 minutes)
EXCERPT	Know where the Bible passages are and have two readers. Leave a little space after each reading. (Less than 10 minutes altogether)
EXPAND	Encourage people to say what they see, hear and feel about the event. This is for comments not discussion. (5-10 minutes)
EXPERIENCE	Leave the individuals space to explore the passage on their own. Some of this they may feel unable to share. (5-10 minutes)
EXPRESS	See if anyone wants to say where they stand in the story – 'I am like so and so' or 'I would like to be like so and so'. (5-10 minutes)
EXPOUND	Allow each member to contribute if they so desire, saying what the reading means to them. (No more than 15 minutes)
EXULT	Keep a short silence and then have the final prayers (5 minutes)
EXPECT	As leader, remind them to look for change and to expect it. (1 minute)

I believe that a group should know before it begins how long the meeting is to last. There is nothing worse than feeling trapped in a meeting that appears endless. The leader must stick to the time schedule, but if people want to stay afterwards that is another matter.

The idea for the title of this book came from one of my Advent prayers called 'Inner Longings'. You may like to make this a prayer of yours throughout this season.

Lord of this world,
we work,
we watch,
we wait for you.
Come down,
come in,
come among us.

Lord of this life,
we labour,
we look,
we long for you.
Come down,
come in,
come among us.

Lord of this second,
we strive,
we serve,
we search for you.
Come down,
come in,
come among us,
that we may dwell in you
and you in us
for ever.
Power Lines (SPCK, 1992)

Prayer can be described as looking and longing for God: giving God our attention with eyes and heart. This calls upon us to be awake to his coming and alert to his call. There is no doubt that God comes to us. The sadness is that we are not ready to make room for him. We have filled our lives with things while the Almighty waits to enter our lives. Think upon these words by St Andrew of Crete (*c.* 660-740):

The one who is present everywhere and fills every thing is

coming. He is coming to fulfil among you the salvation offered to all. Welcome him who welcomed all that pertains to our human nature.

Surely the only response to such thoughts is to say, 'Maranatha!* Come, Lord Jesus.'

Let us make this our theme this Advent.

---

* An Aramaic word used often by the early Christians (1 Corinthians 16:22 and Revelation 22:20), meaning 'Come, Lord'.

14

WEEK 1
Hiding and seeking

EXTRACT

Keep at least a minute of silence (in semi-darkness?)
Light one candle

Pray
Come, my Lord,
my light, my way;
come, my lantern,
night and day;
come, healer,
make me whole.
Come, my Saviour,
protect my soul;
come, my King,
enter my heart;
come, Prince of Peace,
and never depart.
The Open Gate, David Adam (SPCK, 1994)

May the bright light of Christ enlighten our hearts,
shine in our minds and direct our journeying,
and give light to the world

Maranatha! Come, Lord Jesus.

Sing or listen to one of the following:
- God is love, his the care *(216)**
- Love divine, all loves excelling *(428)*

EXCERPT

If possible, have two readers and leave a minute's gap between the readings.

Adam and Eve in hiding

They heard the sound of the Lord God walking in the garden at the time of the evening breeze, and the man and his wife hid themselves from the presence of the Lord God among the trees of the garden. But the Lord God called to the man, and said to him, 'Where are you?' He said, 'I heard the sound of you in the garden, and I was afraid, because I was naked; and I hid myself.' He said, 'Who told you that you were naked? Have you eaten from the tree of which I commanded you not to eat?' The man said, 'The woman whom you gave to be with me, she gave me fruit from the tree, and I ate.' Then the Lord God said to the woman. 'What is this that you have done?' The woman said, 'The serpent tricked me, and I ate.'

Genesis 3:8-13

Mary at the house of Simon the Pharisee

One of the Pharisees asked Jesus to eat with him, and he went into the Pharisee's house and took his place at the table. And a woman in the city, who was a sinner, having learned that he was eating in the Pharisee's house, brought an alabaster jar of ointment. She stood behind him at his feet, weeping, and began to bathe his feet with her tears and to dry them with her hair. Then she continued kissing his feet and anointing them with the ointment. Now when the Pharisee who had invited

---

* All hymn numbers refer to *Complete Anglican Hymns Old and New*, published by Kevin Mayhew.

him saw it, he said to himself, 'If this man were a prophet, he would have known who and what kind of woman this is who is touching him – that she is a sinner.' Jesus spoke up and said to him, 'Simon, I have something to say to you.' 'Teacher,' he replied, 'speak.' 'A certain creditor had two debtors; one owed five hundred denarii, and the other fifty. When they could not pay, he cancelled the debts for both of them. Now which of them will love him more?' Simon answered, 'I suppose the one for whom he cancelled the greater debt.' And Jesus said to him, 'You have judged rightly.' Then turning towards the woman, he said to Simon, 'Do you see this woman? I entered your house; you gave me no water for my feet, but she has bathed my feet with her tears and dried them with her hair. You gave me no kiss, but from the time I came in she has not stopped kissing my feet. You did not anoint my head with oil, but she has anointed my feet with ointment. Therefore, I tell you, her sins, which were many, have been forgiven; hence she has shown great love. But the one to whom little is forgiven, loves little.' Then he said to her. 'Your sins are forgiven.' But those who were at the table with him began to say among themselves. 'Who is this who even forgives sins?' And he said to the woman, 'Your faith has saved you; go in peace.'

Luke 7:36-50

EXPAND

A child once said to me, 'Doing naughty things is not bad, getting caught is!' Picture yourself in Eden. You have done the one thing you were asked not to do. How do you feel? Do you really think you can hide from God? In Jeremiah 23:24 God asks, 'Can anyone hide in a dark corner without my seeing them? Do you not know I fill heaven and earth?' God comes to you, seeks you; are you aware of his coming? What do you see when, in hiding, you have closed so much of reality out? Are your ears tuned to listening to his call? To hear him is to obey; do you really want to hear? Is

17

there some place where God will not find you? Have you lost touch with him? As for taste and smell, perhaps there is the taste of evil, plus excitement mingled with the smell of fear.

Enter the house of Simon the Pharisee and see the cool reception Jesus receives. Compare this with the hot tears of Mary. Listen to the guests complain as they distance themselves and watch Mary wipe Jesus' feet with her hair. They make no real contact. Mary is in touch with Jesus. There is no warmth, or personal relationship from the Pharisees; if anything, there is antagonism. Mary's reaction is warm and loving, making personal contact. They feel the whole affair gets up their nose. Mary fills the room with a beautiful scent. The self-righteous hide their feelings and know nothing of forgiveness. Mary comes to Jesus and knows love, acceptance and forgiveness.

What would your reaction be if this woman gatecrashed your party? What would the guests think of this loose woman in your house?

EXPERIENCE

Spend the next few minutes deciding whether you are hiding from God or coming to him in love. Do you trust that God will forgive, that God will accept you as you are? Are there people you consider to be outside God's grace and goodness? Are you willing to open your life to God that he may be able to come to you? Are you in contact with God?

EXPRESS

Do you see yourself in the stories or are you in fact a mixture of all the different people? At what stage do you see yourself now? Jesus has promised that whoever comes to him he will in no way cast out. Even when people hide from God, he sees them and comes to them.

What are the ways you use to keep in contact with God who comes to you?

EXPOUND

The story of Adam and Eve is our story. It is about how we react, and about our relationship with God. God did not create us out of nothing; he created us out of his love and for his love. God wants a loving relationship with each of us. If we cannot be trusted, we break that relationship. It is amazing how easily we are all tempted. If I left you in a room full of books and told you to look at any book you like except the one on the table, how that book would torment you! Many of us would at least steal a look to see what it is about! We also seek to pass the blame for our situation on to others, Adam blamed Eve, Eve blamed the serpent. More interesting is how we hide from God; we pretend that God does not see or know what we do. In hiding we are trying to keep God out of our lives. God will seek us out and will ask us, 'Where are you?' I am sure the following extract from the poem 'Hound of heaven' will be meaningful to most in the group:

I fled him, down the nights and down the days;
I fled him down the arches of the years;
I fled him, down the labyrinthine ways
of my own mind; and in the mist of tears
I hid from him, and under running laughter.
Up vistaed hopes I sped;
and shot, precipitated,
adown titanic glooms of chasmed fears,
from those strong feet that followed, followed after.
But with unhurrying chase,
and unperturbed pace,
deliberate speed, majestic instancy,
they beat – and a voice beat
more instant than the feet –
'All things betray thee, who betrayest me.'
Francis Thompson

Let someone read this poem, especially if it speaks strongly to anyone.

It is important to be aware of the situation caused by this woman, who was an outcast of decent society, coming into Simon's home. All the good-living people were shocked and thought that Jesus should have known better than to encourage her. In Palestine no respectable woman would be seen in public with her hair unbound. On the day she was married, a girl would have her hair bound up and would not be seen again with loose hair. To appear with flowing tresses of hair is to advertise the looseness of her way of living; it suggests someone of immoral earnings. The 'ointment' was no doubt the scent she used to lure men to her, likely to be seen as an aphrodisiac. Now notice how steamy this event must have looked. Jesus is well aware of the tears that fall on to him as he sits on the floor, big hot drops falling on his feet. The woman, no doubt heavily scented, kneels down and kisses his feet over and over again. She wipes his feet with her hair, those soft tresses acting as a towel. Then she breaks open the scent and pours it over Jesus; the whole room smells of it. Take time and look: is this the holy Jesus you know? This is the friend of publicans and sinners beyond doubt. What a contrast: the 'church' people invited him but made no real contact; the woman comes to him as she is, and finds forgiveness and peace. Above all, we see grace at work, the free and unearned gift of God himself offered to the woman who came to him. We cannot earn a relationship with any person; it is their free gift to give. To buy a relationship is to treat someone as if they were in the same trade as this woman. Gifts are to be an expression of our love, not to purchase that love. God gives us his love while we are yet sinners. All that God asks in return is that we give our love to him. Some people even blame their way of life for not coming to God.

EXULT

Give thanks that Jesus comes to you just as you are. He does not wait until you change: he does give you the opportunity for change and for newness of life.

Listen to or have read one of the following hymns:
- Just as I am without one plea *(374)*
- Come, my Lord, my light, my way *(The Open Gate,* David Adam)
- Come, thou long-expected Jesus *(128)*

Prayers

Dear Jesus,
help me to spread your fragrance everywhere I go.
Flood my soul with your spirit and life.
Penetrate and possess my whole being so utterly
that my life may be only a radiance of yours.
Stay with me, and then I shall begin to shine as you shine,
so to shine as to be light to others;
the light, O Jesus, will be all from you,
none of it will be mine;
it will be you, shining on others through me.
Let me thus praise you in the way that you love best,
by shining on those around me.
John Henry Newman (1801-1890)

Come, Lord Jesus,
when this world is as dark as night,
you are the One we call the light.
Come, Lord Jesus.

When we are tempted to go astray
you are the One we call the way.
Come, Lord Jesus.

When we are falling in the strife
you are the One who is the life.
Come, Lord Jesus.

When troubles to our lives bring harm
you are the One who brings us calm.
Come, Lord Jesus.

(*This could be sung – see* Music from Lindisfarne, *published by Kevin Mayhew)*

May the Lord in his coming
find us looking, longing and loving.

EXPECT

Expect your God to seek you out this week. Make space for him in your time and home. Do not hide in busyness; come to him as you are, open your life to him. Say regularly, 'Maranatha! Come, Lord Jesus.'

The leader should give the crib figures Joseph and Mary, plus a candle to a member of the group to take home. If there are no crib figures, a drawing of Joseph and Mary would do. It may be possible for the figures to be put up for one night, then passed on to another member of the group so that they travel around. This is to express our openness to others and to the coming of our Lord. Let each home say a welcome and a prayer to Jesus. With children sing or say 'Away in a manger'. Say especially:

Be near me, Lord Jesus;
I ask thee to stay
close by me for ever,
and love me, I pray.
Bless all the dear children
in thy tender care,
and fit us for heaven,
to live with thee there.

WEEK 2
Seeking and finding

EXTRACT

Keep at least a minute of silence (in semi-darkness?)
Light two candles

Pray

Christ as a light illumine and guide me.
Christ as a shield overshadow me.
Christ be under me, Christ be over me.
Christ on my right and on my left.
Christ this day before and behind me.
Christ be within and all around me.
Christ as a light illumine and guide me.

Attributed to St Patrick

May the bright light of Christ enlighten our hearts,
shine in our minds and direct our journeying,
and give light to the world.

Maranatha! Come, Lord Jesus.

Sing or listen to one of the following:

* O come, O come, Emmanuel *(480)*
* One more step along the world I go *(525)*

EXCERPT

If possible, have two readers and leave a minute's gap between the readings.

Abram leaves Ur

Now the Lord said to Abram, 'Go from your country and your kindred and your father's house to the land that I will show you. I will make of you a great nation, and I will bless you, and make your name great, so that you will be a blessing. I will bless those who bless you, and the one who curses you I will curse; and in you all the families of the earth shall be blessed.'

So Abram went, as the Lord had told him; and Lot went with him. Abram was seventy-five years old when he departed from Haran. Abram took his wife Sarai and his brother's son Lot, and all the possessions that they had gathered, and the persons whom they had acquired in Haran; and they set forth to go to the land of Canaan. When they had come to the land of Canaan, Abram passed through the land to the place at Shechem, to the oak of Moreh. At that time the Canaanites were in the land. Then the Lord appeared to Abram, and said, 'To your offspring I will give this land.' So he built there an altar to the Lord, who had appeared to him. From there he moved on to the hill country on the east of Bethel, and pitched his tent, with Bethel on the west and Ai on the east; and there he built an altar to the Lord and invoked the name of the Lord. And Abram journeyed on by stages toward the Negeb.

Genesis 12:1-9

Zacchaeus meets Jesus

He entered Jericho and was passing through it. A man was there named Zacchaeus; he was a chief tax collector and was rich. He was trying to see who Jesus was, but on account of the crowd he could not, because he was short in stature. So he ran ahead and climbed a sycamore tree to see him, because he was going to pass that way. When Jesus came to the place, he looked up and said to him, 'Zacchaeus, hurry and come down; for I must stay at your house today.' So he hurried down and was happy to welcome him. All who saw it began to grumble and said, 'He has gone to be the guest of one who is a sinner.' Zacchaeus stood there and said to the Lord, 'Look, half of my possessions, Lord, I will give to the poor; and if I have defrauded anyone of anything, I will pay back four times as much.' Then Jesus said to him, 'Today salvation has come to this house, because he too is a son of Abraham. For the Son of Man came to seek out and to save the lost.'

Luke 19:1-10

EXPAND

Abram was of an age when he should have left home long ago. At the age of 75 it is a little late to leave his father's house and family. It is always hard to leave home, to leave our safety and security. All are called to venture; we all need to move out at some time. How do you relate to Abram? Is there something that is calling you, making you restless? Telling you there is more to life than what you have at the moment? What do you see Abram doing in preparation to move out? How do you feel about going into the unknown?

Zacchaeus did not move very far but it was a courageous leap in his character. An important official climbing a tree, it must have made the crowd laugh. What did it take for this rich man to risk making a fool of himself? Do our own fears, pride or unwillingness to change hold us back? As living beings, we are called to move and change and grow. What are the reasons we give for not changing?

EXPERIENCE

Explore your own life and its moments of change and risk. What changes were forced upon you and how did you cope? Always in our lives there are areas ready for change. Explore those in the silence and see if you are ready to venture.

25

EXPRESS

The need to move and change is part of our lives. Do you see yourself in the story of Abram? Perhaps you feel you have left it too late to change – Abram waited until he was 75 before venturing. Do you feel in your heart a restlessness that is seeking to make you alter your way of life?

In the story of Zacchaeus you might want to align yourself with the onlookers rather than Zacchaeus, with those who laugh at the risk-takers and adventurers. Are you willing to look the fool for Christ's sake?

Where do you see yourself in the story of these two risk-takers?

EXPOUND

The world has a great admiration for those who have 'arrived', who have 'made it'. This usually means people of achievement, who have reached some peak or pinnacle. This is a good thing to admire but they had to work, to move, to exert themselves to get there. Once a person reaches a goal, if they are still alive, they will work towards another. It took Abram a long time to move out, and even when he left he did not know where he was going. His was a walk into the dark. Perhaps it was the need for land, for food, for a place to call his own. Whatever it was, it had created a restlessness. The scriptures look deeper. It was not just events; it was God calling him through the events. It was God who said to Abram, 'Leave your country, your family and your father's house for the land I will show you' (Genesis 12:1). God speaks to us through our own being and the events about us. The writer of the letter to the Hebrews takes this a step further: 'It was by faith that Abraham obeyed the call to set out for a country that was the inheritance given to him and his descendants, and that he set out not knowing where he was going' (Hebrews 11:8).

Faith is not what we believe; it is a relationship with God, a personal living relationship. Faith does not deal with a God of history, but with a God who is here and with us now. Faith is not

26

credal statements; it is how we live in the presence of God. Remember, the devil believes. Ours is a living faith. Abram is seen as the father of faith because he went out in the presence and power of God. He did not know where he was going but he knew who was going with him. In all our journeying, if we are to survive, we need to seek and know the presence of God.

Stop for a moment and affirm, 'The Lord is here; his Spirit is with us.'

Zacchaeus was a little man with a big appetite. He may have been small but he had great longings. He sought riches and power, and he gained them. He was one of the richest men in Jericho, but he was not liked. Zak, as they called him, was a horrible character, not likeable in any way. He was only interested in making money. Some said he was the lowest man in town and Jericho was the very bottom. Not only was Jericho a place of wickedness and vice, it was also the lowest town in the world at 700 feet below sea level. It could be said he was the lowest man in the lowest town in the world; you could not get any lower, and Jesus came to him!

Zacchaeus was a tax collector by profession, which meant he worked for the Romans, the enemy that occupied the country. As a consequence, he was banned from places of worship; he did not go to church. He made his fortune by being the chief inspector of taxes. Anything that moved, Zak taxed, anything on legs that came into the city, any food, any produce. All had to pay tax, from which he took his cut, and no one liked him. He worked on the Sabbath. They said he had no friends except people like him; that is, until Jesus came. The other side of Zacchaeus was a deep emptiness that nothing could fill; he had money, position, a good home, but he was not satisfied. Zacchaeus knew there was more to life than what he owned. In his own way he was discovering the words of Jesus: 'A person's life does not consist in the abundance of things he possesses.' The same inner longing would make Augustine of Hippo write, 'Lord, our hearts are restless until they rest in you.' It was this inner emptiness that made Zacchaeus go out to meet Jesus. Many of the crowd did not know their need. The inner longing of Zacchaeus drove him to put aside pride and position and to come to Jesus. As he was open to change, Jesus came to him and stayed with him. As ever the crowd complained that Jesus was found with sinners. Sometimes the Church still fails to see that this is the reason Jesus came to earth, for the sake of sinners. Zacchaeus responds to Jesus and becomes a changed man. He now gives away and recompenses people that he cheated. More than all of this, the emptiness has gone; he has a new relationship. Jesus recognises this and calls him a 'son of Abraham'. Zacchaeus is also a man of faith. It is well to take to heart the last sentence in the story of Zacchaeus: 'Today salvation has come to his house, because this too is a son of Abraham: for the Son of Man has come to seek out and save what was lost.' Not only do we need to seek a relationship with Jesus, he seeks to have a relationship with us.

Zacchaeus needed a friend and he found a true friend in Jesus.

(Let the group discuss this for about 12 minutes)

You may like to get someone to read these words of Augustine of Hippo before or after the discussion:

I was slow to love you, Lord,
your age old beauty is still new to me:
I was slow to love you!
You were within me,
yet I stayed outside
seeking you there;
in my ugliness I grabbed at
the beautiful things of your creation.
Already you were with me,
but I was still far from you.
The things of this world kept me away:
I did not know then
that if they had not existed through you
they would not have existed at all.
Then you called me
and your cry overcame my deafness.

You shone out
and your light overcame my blindness.
You surrounded me with your fragrance
and I breathed it in,
so that I now yearn for more of you;
I tasted you
and now I am hungry and thirsty for you;
you touched me
and now I burn with a longing for your peace.

EXULT

Give thanks that Jesus comes to you just as you are. He does not
wait until you change: he does give you the opportunity for
change and for newness of life. Rejoice that 'by faith we are saved'
– not by beliefs, not by the Church, but by a living relationship
with our God.

Pray

God of all love and beauty,
open our hearts to welcome you,
that your Son Jesus Christ, in his coming,
may find us looking and longing for him
and may find in us a dwelling prepared for himself:
who is alive and reigns with you and the Holy Spirit,
One God now and for ever.

O God, from whom to turn is to fall,
to whom to turn is to rise,
and in whom to abide is to live for ever:
grant us in all our duties your help,
in all our confusions your guidance,
in all our dangers your protection,

and in all our sorrows your peace;
through Jesus Christ our Lord.
Augustine (354-430)

Sing or read one of the following:
- Come, thou long-expected Jesus *(128)*
- What a friend we have in Jesus *(727)*
- The God of Abraham praise *(642)*

EXPECT

Expect to meet him on the way. Know that wherever you are, whatever you do, God today desires to have a relationship with you. Expect your friendship with God to grow this day. Say quietly throughout the week ahead:

Lord, we look for you. We long for you.
Maranatha! Come, Lord Jesus.

Send out Joseph and Mary (see Week 1).

WEEK 3
Finding and seeing

EXTRACT

Keep at least a minute of silence (in semi-darkness?)
Light three candles

Pray

O Christ, our Morning Star,
Splendour of light eternal,
shining with the glory of the rainbow,
come and awaken us
from the greyness of our apathy
and renew us in your gift of hope.

Bede (673-735)

Open our eyes this day to your presence
that we may know that we dwell in you
and be aware that you are in us.
Grant us a glimpse of your great glory,
as we desire you and seek your love.
As we seek, grant us to find,
as we find, grant us to be found by you;
through Christ our Lord who comes this day.

May the bright light of Christ enlighten our hearts,
shine in our minds and direct our journeying,
and give light to the world.

Maranatha! Come, Lord Jesus

Sing or listen to one of the following:
- Amazing grace *(29)*
- Rise and shine *(883)*
- Thou didst leave thy throne *(683)*

EXCERPT

If possible, have two readers and leave a minute's gap between the readings.

Jacob's dream

Jacob left Beer-sheba and went towards Haran. He came to a certain place and stayed there for the night, because the sun had set. Taking one of the stones of the place, he put it under his head and lay down in that place. And he dreamed that there was a ladder set up on the earth, the top of it reaching to heaven; and the angels of God were ascending and descending on it. And the Lord stood beside him and said, 'I am the Lord, the God of Abraham your father and the God of Isaac; the land on which you lie I will give to you and to your offspring; and your offspring shall be like the dust of the earth, and you shall spread abroad to the west and to the east and to the north and to the south; and all the families of the earth shall be blessed in you and in your offspring. Know that I am with you and will keep you wherever you go, and will bring you back to this land; for I will not leave you until I have done what I have promised you.' Then Jacob woke from his sleep and said, 'Surely the Lord is in this place – and I did not know it!' And he was afraid, and said, 'How awesome is this place! This is none other than the house of God, and this is the gate of heaven.'

Genesis 28:10-17

The blind man and Jesus

As he walked along, he saw a man blind from birth. His disciples asked him, 'Rabbi, who sinned, this man or his parents, that he was born blind?' Jesus answered, 'Neither this man nor his parents sinned; he was born blind so that God's works might be revealed in him. We must work the works of him who sent me while it is day; night is coming when no one can work. As long as I am in the world, I am the light of the world.' When he had said this, he spat on the ground and made mud with the saliva and spread the mud on the man's eyes, saying to him. 'Go, wash in the pool of Siloam' (which means Sent). Then he went and washed and came back able to see. The neighbours and those who had seen him before as a beggar began to ask, 'Is this not the man who used to sit and beg?' Some were saying, 'It is he.' Others were saying, 'No, but it is someone like him.' He kept saying, 'I am the man.' But they kept asking him, 'Then how were your eyes opened?' He answered, 'The man called Jesus made mud, spread it on my eyes, and said to me, "Go to Siloam and wash." Then I went and washed and received my sight.' They said to him, 'Where is he?' He said, 'I do not know.' . . . So for the second time they called the man who had been blind, and they said to him, 'Give glory to God! We know that this man is a sinner.' He answered. 'I do not know whether he is a sinner. One thing I do know, that though I was blind, now I see.'

John 9:1-12, 24-25

EXPAND

The Jacob story is about a man's awakening to the reality of the presence of God. How do you think he felt as he awoke from his dream? Would the world ever be the same again? What would you see him doing after such a dream? Would you let such an event change your life?

Someone once remarked, 'Many creatures are born blind; it is only men that never open their eyes.' And they meant men only, not women! The man born blind from birth obviously found life restricting; there were many things he could not do because he could not see. Like other people who are blind, he would have developed his other senses. Do you use all your senses? Can you say, 'I once was blind but now I see'?

EXPERIENCE

Do we have a recurring dream that disturbs us, or a regular thought or desire that wants us to change? Are we sure we are truly awake to what is going on around us?

Perhaps some may like to talk about a moment in their life that changed their way of seeing and thinking for ever. The blind Bartimaeus was aware that Jesus of Nazareth was passing by and made contact with him. The crowd looked on and let him pass by. Are we awake to Jesus, aware of him, as he comes to us? (Mark 10:46-52)

Let people think this over on their own for about five minutes.

EXPRESS

Where do people see themselves in this story? Do they feel like Jacob before he awoke, in the dark and unsure of what to do? Perhaps they can tell of a moment, a vision that changed their lives. Many visions are not dramatic, but a gradual opening of the eyes to reality; others can be as startling as Saul's conversion on the road to Damascus. It is interesting that Saul's vision left him blind for a while. Can we do anything to help in the opening of our eyes? We might like to blame our blindness on events around us, on our parents, on sin, but when the Light of the World comes to us he offers to open our eyes.

Do we truly want to see and to be aware of the coming of

Christ? Can we rejoice with John Newton, the writer of 'Amazing grace', and say:

Amazing grace, how sweet the sound
that found a wretch like me.
I once was lost but now am found,
was blind but now I see.

EXPOUND

In the nineteenth century Edwin Abbot wrote a book about the flatlands. It is the story about a two-dimensional world, a world that has length and breadth but no height. It may sound a strange world but are you sure you live in a world that has height and depth to it? Too often, like the flatlanders, we live our lives on a level with no higher reaches. Flatlanders never look upwards.

Jacob seems to have lived in the flatlands. He was out to get what he could for himself. His mother even helped him to cheat on his father and brother. He created such a difficult situation at home that he had to leave. It would seem that Jacob was out for himself. We meet him alone, in the dark, tired and no doubt homesick. His flatland views would take him no further than this; if he would keep going he would fall over the edge! What could he do but stop and sleep? Under a starry sky, he camped down with a stone for his pillow. It was here at a place that would be called Bethel, the House of God, that his life and world would take on a new dimension. In the night Jacob's vision widened. He saw the heights to which he was called to ascend. He saw there was a stairway to heaven. He was not alone. He was called to higher things; God entered into his way of thinking and his life. He awoke out of his long sleep and said, 'Surely, the Lord is in this place and I did not know it.' It is when we find one holy place that all places become holy; when we find God, or God finds us, in one place that we discover his presence everywhere. Then our eyes and our hearts are opened.

Remember the words of Francis Thompson:

> O World invisible, we view thee,
> O World intangible, we touch thee,
> O World unknowable, we know thee,
> inapprehensible, we clutch thee!
>
> The angels keep their ancient places –
> turn but a stone, and start a wing!
> 'Tis ye, 'tis your estranged faces,
> that miss the many-splendoured thing.

There are not two separate worlds; heaven and earth are one. Our eyes prevent us from seeing the fullness and the richness of our world. We need to have our eyes opened until we can say with Julian of Norwich, 'We are more in heaven than earth.'

The man blind from birth could not explain his ability to see. Too often, like the church people in this story, we seek to discuss the hows and wherefores and fail to rejoice in the gift of vision itself. Vision defies analysis; its proof is in its use. Do we go into church to give thanks for our sight and our insight? Rejoice like the blind man: 'I once was blind but now I see.'

EXULT

Give thanks that Jesus comes to you just as you are. He does not wait until you change: he does give you the opportunity for change and for newness of life.

> Lord, open our eyes to your presence:
> Open our ears to your call.
> Open our lips to sing your praises.
> Open our hearts to your great love.
> May we awaken out of sleep
> that we may be aware of you,
> glimpse at your great glory
> and enjoy your presence.

Sing or listen to one of the following:
- As Jacob with travel was weary one day *(775)*
- O Love that wilt not let me go *(517)*

EXPECT

Expect to meet your God in the day that lies ahead. Lie down at night in his presence saying quietly, 'Surely, the Lord is in this place.' Let your house become a Bethel, a house of God. Throughout the day say:

> Lord, we look for you. We long for you.
> Open our eyes to your presence.
> Maranatha! Come, Lord Jesus.

Send out Mary and Joseph (see Week 1).

WEEK 4
Seeing and worshipping

EXTRACT

Keep at least a minute of silence (in semi-darkness?)
Light four candles

Pray
Come, true light.
Come, life eternal.
Come, hidden mystery.
Come, treasure without name.
Come, reality beyond all words.
Come, person beyond all understanding.
Come, rejoicing without end.
Come, light that knows no evening.
Come, unfailing expectation of the saved.
Come, raising of the fallen.
Come, resurrection of the dead.
Come, all-powerful, for unceasingly you create,
refashion and change all things by your will alone.
Come, invisible whom none may touch and handle.
Come, for you continue always unmoved,
yet at every instant you are wholly in movement;
you draw near to us who lie in hell,
yet you remain higher than the heavens.
Come, for your name fills our hearts with longing
and is ever on our lips; yet who you are and what your nature is,
we cannot say or know.
Come, Alone to the alone.

Come, for you are yourself the desire that is within me.
Come, the consolation of my humble soul.
Come, my joy, my endless delight.
Symeon the New Theologian (949-1022)

May the bright light of Christ enlighten our hearts,
shine in our minds and direct our journeying,
and give light to the world

Maranatha! Come, Lord Jesus.

Listen to or sing one of the following:
• Be still, for the presence of the Lord *(67)*
• Come, my Lord, my light, my way (*The Open Gate*, David Adam)

EXCERPT

If possible, have two readers and leave a minute's gap between the readings.

Moses and the burning bush

Moses was keeping the flock of his father-in-law Jethro, the priest of Midian; he led his flock beyond the wilderness, and came to Horeb, the mountain of God. There the angel of the Lord appeared to him in a flame of fire out of a bush; he looked, and the bush was blazing, yet it was not consumed. Then Moses said, 'I must turn aside and look at this great sight, and see why the bush is not burned up.' When the Lord saw that he had turned aside to see, God called to him out of the bush. 'Moses, Moses!' And he said, 'Here I am.' Then he said, 'Come no closer! Remove the sandals from your feet, for the place on which you are standing is holy ground.' He said further,

'I am the God of your father, the God of Abraham, the God of Isaac, and the God of Jacob.' And Moses hid his face, for he was afraid to look at God.

Then the Lord said, 'I have observed the misery of my people who are in Egypt; I have heard their cry on account of their taskmasters. Indeed, I know their sufferings, and I have come down to deliver them from the Egyptians, and to bring them up out of that land to a good and broad land, a land flowing with milk and honey, to the country of the Canaanites, the Hittites, the Amorites, the Perizzites, the Hivites, and the Jebusites. The cry of the Israelites has now come to me; I have also seen how the Egyptians oppress them. So come, I will send you to Pharaoh to bring my people, the Israelites, out of Egypt.' But Moses said to God, 'Who am I that I should go to Pharaoh, and bring the Israelites out of Egypt?' He said, 'I will be with you; and this shall be the sign for you that it is I who sent you; when you have brought the people out of Egypt, you shall worship God on this mountain.'

Exodus 3:1-12

The Transfiguration

Now about eight days after these sayings Jesus took with him Peter and John and James, and went up on the mountain to pray. And while he was praying, the appearance of his face changed, and his clothes became dazzling white. Suddenly they saw two men, Moses and Elijah, talking to him. They appeared in glory and were speaking of his departure, which he was about to accomplish at Jerusalem. Now Peter and his companions were weighed down with sleep; but since they had stayed awake, they saw his glory and the two men who stood with him. Just as they were leaving him, Peter said to Jesus, 'Master, it is good for us to be here; let us make three dwellings, one for you, one for Moses, and one for Elijah' – not knowing what he said. While he was saying this, a cloud came and overshadowed them; and they were terrified as they entered the cloud. Then from the cloud came a voice that said, 'This is my Son, my Chosen; listen to him!' When the voice had spoken, Jesus was found alone. And they kept silent and in those days told no one any of the things they had seen.

Luke 9:28-36

EXPAND

The burning bush and the transfiguration experience of the disciples defy explanation: both are about the otherness of God. Let individuals say what they think happened to Moses. What did he see and feel? How do the group react to the mysterious and the unknown? Can it all be scientifically explained? Do people feel there are events and experiences that are beyond normal descriptions? How would they react to a fire that seems to have no source and a voice from the emptiness around them?

What do you think about the experience of the disciples on the mountain? Would you have liked to have been there, and what comments would you have made? Peter's comments sound a little inept! (Remember these are just comments; avoid discussion.)

EXPERIENCE

Can anyone relate to the experience of Moses in the desert? There is no doubt we have desert experiences, times when our plans fall apart, times of emptiness. Have we seen such times as openings, as emptying out to make room for God? The transfiguration of Jesus is a putting into words of what is beyond the powers of description. There are some events too wonderful to press into words. Have a moment or two of silence and give thanks for life-enriching experiences. Remember that people cannot share what they feel they cannot express. (As usual let this whole time last for 5-10 minutes.)

EXPRESS

There are times when we are in the desert and experience nothing. There are times when the road is uphill all the way and we feel we are on the mountainside. But in these periods there are often glimpses of the 'other', of a far horizon. Do we see these experiences as expressions of what happens in our lives?

Members of the group may like to say if they see either of these stories as having a link with their own experiences in life.

EXPOUND

The story of Moses sounded idyllic. From an endangered infancy to being raised like a prince in the palace, this seemed to be a story of rags to riches. But he felt solidarity with his own oppressed people and this brought him into conflict. Soon Moses had to escape for his life. From the life of riches, he became a desert wanderer. From the activities of the royal court, he entered the deep silence of the desert. The writer to the Hebrews sees this all as part of a greater plan:

> It was faith that made Moses, when he had grown up, refuse to be called the son of the king's daughter. He preferred to suffer with God's people rather than enjoy sin for a little while. He reckoned that to suffer scorn for the Messiah was worth far more than all the treasures of Egypt, for he kept his eyes on the future reward.
>
> *Hebrews 11:24-26*

It was in the emptiness, in the silence, that Moses became aware of the call and the presence of God. In the desert Moses worshipped his Creator on holy ground.

You do not have to go to church to find God. This is so true: God is everywhere, waiting to break into our lives. If we make space, if we make room for him, he comes (not that he has ever been away!). Holy ground is all around us! All places and all things have the potential of revealing his presence. God is in the whole world and the world is in God. The Holy, the utterly other, waits to find entrance into our closed lives. The burning bush is the call to adventure, to a life-changing experience, and to discovering that our God is with us, comes to us and calls us. As God comes, let him find us alert, looking and longing for him.

The Transfiguration is not so much a change in Jesus as in the perception of his disciples. There on the mountain their eyes were open, just like Jacob's. They saw Jesus clearly as he truly is. They saw that he was more than a man, more than a good preacher. They suddenly knew that he was the One who fulfilled the Law, as incorporated in Moses, and the prophets, as incorporated in Elijah. They knew in themselves that he was and is the Messiah, the Holy One of God. Note that Luke says, 'Peter and his companions were sound asleep but when they woke up they saw Jesus' glory' (Luke 9:32). Can we really believe they fell asleep climbing up the mountain? It is possible but it is more likely that Luke is talking of a spiritual awakening. In these events there is a challenge to our way of seeing and our vision; both events are a call to worship God.

EXULT

Give thanks that Jesus comes to you just as you are. He does not wait until you change: he does give you the opportunity for change and for newness of life.

> You, Lord, are in this place;
> it is a holy place
> for your presence fills it.
> Your presence is peace.
>
> You, Lord, are in my heart;
> it is a holy place,
> your presence fills it.
> Your presence is love.

Sing or listen to one of the following:
* Will you come and follow me *(752)*
* Moses, I know you're the man *(451)*

EXPECT
Expect to meet the utterly Other, the great God, today and throughout the week. Say throughout the day:

Come to my heart, Lord Jesus,
there is room in my heart for you.
Maranatha! Come, Lord Jesus.

Send out Joseph and Mary (see Week 1).

WEEK 5

Worshipping and obeying

EXTRACT
Keep at least a minute of silence (in semi-darkness?)
Light five candles

Pray
O thou who camest from above,
the pure celestial fire to impart,
kindle a flame of sacred love
on the mean altar of my heart.

There let it for thy glory burn
with inextinguishable blaze,
and trembling to its source return
in humble prayer and fervent praise.
Charles Wesley (1707-1788)

Come, Lord, be known among us.
As you came to earth, born of Mary,
come into our hearts and homes.

Come, Lord, be known among us.
As you became a little child,
help us to grow in awareness of you.

Come, Lord, be known among us.
As you walked this earth,
help us to walk and work with you.

May the bright light of Christ enlighten our hearts,
shine in our mind, direct our journeying,
and scatter the darkness from the world.

Maranatha! Come, Lord Jesus.

Play or sing one of the following:
- O little town of Bethlehem *(508)*
- Tell out, my soul, the greatness of the Lord *(631)*

EXCERPT

If possible, have two readers and leave a minute's gap between the readings.

Isaiah's vision in the Temple

In the year that King Uzziah died, I saw the Lord sitting on a throne, high and lofty; and the hem of his robe filled the temple. Seraphs were in attendance above him; each had six wings; with two they covered their faces, and with two they covered their feet, and with two they flew. And one called to another and said:

'Holy, holy, holy is the Lord of hosts; the whole earth is full of his glory.'

The pivots on the thresholds shook at the voices of those who called, and the house filled with smoke. And I said: 'Woe is me! I am lost, for I am a man of unclean lips, and I live among a people of unclean lips; yet my eyes have seen the King, the Lord of hosts!'

Then one of the seraphs flew to me, holding a live coal that had been taken from the altar with a pair of tongs. The seraph touched my mouth with it and said: 'Now that this has touched your lips, your guilt has departed and your sin is blotted out.' Then I heard the voice of the Lord saying. 'Whom shall I send, and who will go for us?' And I said, 'Here am I; send me!'

Isaiah 6:1-8

The Annunciation and the 'Yes' of Mary

In the sixth month the angel Gabriel was sent by God to a town in Galilee called Nazareth, to a virgin engaged to a man whose name was Joseph, of the house of David. The virgin's name was Mary. And he came to her and said, 'Greetings, favoured one! The Lord is with you.' But she was much perplexed by his words and pondered what sort of greeting this might be. The angel said to her, 'Do not be afraid, Mary, for you have found favour with God. And now, you will conceive in your womb and bear a son, and you will name him Jesus. He will be great, and will be called the Son of the Most High, and the Lord God will give to him the throne of his ancestor David. He will reign over the house of Jacob for ever, and of his kingdom there will be no end.' Mary said to the angel, 'How can this be, since I am a virgin?' The angels said to her, 'The Holy Spirit will come upon you, and the power of the Most High will overshadow you; therefore the child to be born will be holy; he will be called Son of God. And now, your relative Elizabeth in her old age has also conceived a son; and this is the sixth month for her who was said to be barren. For nothing will be impossible with God.' Then Mary said, 'Here am I, the servant of the Lord; let it be with me according to your word.' Then the angel departed from her.

Luke 1:26-38

EXPAND

What do you see happening to Isaiah in the throne room of the Temple? Can you put into other words what you think he heard and saw? It was not just in his mind. The word 'holy' is almost beyond description; it describes something or someone that is totally beyond our comprehension. What word would you use to describe the sudden awareness of God in your life?

Mary appears as no one important, a young countrywoman going about her own business. Suddenly this other dimension breaks in. We are in the realm of angels, the overshadowing Spirit and the promised Son of God. Mary's reaction is to say, 'Be it unto me according to your word.' She offered her obedience. Only those who obey the king are truly part of the kingdom. Her other reaction is to praise God. There is every chance that Mary's Song arose out of her knowing and meditating on Hannah's song (1 Samuel 2:1-10). Maybe the angel Gabriel disturbed her meditation! We miss much if we do not know and meditate upon our Scriptures. We need to know and obey the word of God.

EXPERIENCE

How would you have felt if you were Isaiah and your friend and supporter died? It would seem Isaiah's prayers for Uzziah were not answered. There are times when God seems to have left us and we are on our own. Imagine yourself before the empty throne. What are your feelings; how do you react? Continue to stand there and let God enter your life. What can you say now? In the silence come before him and say, 'Holy, holy, holy.' Do not let feelings alone triumph, for God is with you.

Mary was going about her ordinary tasks. In a painting by Elsie Anna Wood, Mary is feeding the hens when the angel Gabriel appears. She was not in church or even in a 'holy place'. Suddenly this other dimension breaks into her daily routine. This other dimension is also part of our lives. Look at your life and see if there are moments when you can say, 'At this turning point my life had another dimension.' Seek to realise the kingdom of heaven is close at hand all the time in your daily life.

EXPRESS

Is anyone able to relate to the experience of Isaiah? Explore the feeling of emptiness and being bereft, as well as vision and hope. Sometimes a life needs to be made insecure, hollowed out, before it can be aware of God and receive him. Does any member of the group see this as relating to their experience? If you had to choose a single word to express God's presence, what would it be?

Worship leads to awareness. Do we actually spend enough time each day resting and rejoicing in the presence of God? Are you in the habit of affirming God's presence throughout the day? Awareness leads to obedience. In affirming his presence, do we offer to live and work for God? Worship, awareness and obedience are what faith is about. Are we seeking to grow in our faith?

EXPOUND

Isaiah is bereft; he has lost his friend and patron, King Uzziah. The throne is empty and the king is dead. There is a great fear that chaos is about to descend upon the kingdom and Isaiah. With the death of the king, Isaiah fears for his future. 'The throne is empty and the king is dead' are words that keep filling Isaiah's mind and heart. Isaiah had prayed in the Temple for the recovery of the king. It is as if God did not hear. Isaiah felt as if he was totally alone. God is dead and the throne is empty: we are like orphans in a chaotic world. T. S. Eliot described our western world as 'a giant orphanage where no one knows his origins and no one ever comes to call for him'. The main theme of Franz Kafka's book *The Castle* is the loneliness and bewilderment of modern man. The village of the castle seems to function as normal. It has its shops, streets, schools and pubs but no one seems to be in control, there is no active leadership. The castle looms over all but there is no communication; perhaps there is nothing up there, perhaps the throne is empty. The feeling of modern people is very like the feeling of Isaiah. In their book *God is no more*, Werner and Lotte Pelz wrote:

God is no more because he has become an idea – a mere word; and this has confined him within neat and tidy systems. He is found at the end of an argument: his nature is formally stated: he is conventionalised, made familiar and respectable – and so he dies.

Again the feeling that the throne is empty, the king is dead.

Into the recurring refrain of emptiness, in the empty throne room of the Temple, into the empty heart of Isaiah, God comes: 'In the year that King Uzziah died, I saw the Lord.' In these few words we are told God has not forsaken his world, he comes to it and into it. Though there are troubles all around and chaos seeks to take over, God is still in control. The throne is not empty for God is on the throne. In the words of St Paul, nothing shall separate us from the love of God in Christ Jesus.

The vision is wonderful but it is only part of the story. Vision is tested by its results. God who comes asks us to join in his work. To Isaiah he says, 'Whom shall I send, who will go for us?' And the response is, 'Here am I, send me.' To hear God is to obey God. To see what God requires means the call to do his will. Think over these words from a prayer card:

A person with a vision
and no task is a dreamer.
A person with a task
and no vision is a drudge.
A person with a vision
and a task is a prophet.

We can only pray 'Your kingdom come' if we live 'Your will be done'. I was once describing the beauties of the world to some schoolchildren when one child piped up, 'He could not have done it without the council', meaning the workers of which his dad was one. Think over that deep statement. The child knew: without us God will not; without God we cannot. God comes as king. Enter into his kingdom by saying, 'Here I am, send me.' Worship and obedience are signs of the kingdom in our lives and in our hearts.

In Mary, God waits to be born. God does not force himself upon this young woman; he waits for her to assent to his coming.

God comes fully when Mary says, 'Yes': 'Be it unto me according to your word.' Here is a young woman engaged to be married, willing to risk all to do the will of God. What risks there must have been to be willing to bear the Christ Child, risks that will go with her for the rest of her life. Mary's assent meant God was invited to dwell among us. The Divine became human that we might share in the Divine. As Christ becomes a child of Mary, we are given the power to be children of God. What was lost through the fall of Adam and Eve has been restored through the obedience of Mary. The Incarnation is a great act in our redemption. As we give thanks for the obedience of Mary, let us remember the best thanksgiving is to say to God, 'Your will be done.'

Mary's song, the Magnificat, has its origins in the first Book of Samuel. We need to learn to use the Scriptures as our guide to worship and obedience. We have to discover personally that the God who comes to Isaiah and to Mary is the God who comes to us. Here are some challenging words from Angelus Silesius:

Though Christ a thousand times
in Bethlehem be born,
if he is not born in you,
you are still forlorn.

Then in this Christmas season take to heart these words:

O Holy child of Bethlehem,
descend to us, we pray;
cast out our sin, and enter in,
be born in us today.
We hear the Christmas angels
the great glad tidings tell:
O come to us, abide with us,
Our Lord Emmanuel.

Phillips Brooks (1835-1893)

51

EXULT

Give thanks that Jesus comes to you just as you are. He does not wait until you change: he does give you the opportunity for change and for newness of life.

Sing or play one of the following:
- O come all ye faithful *(479)*
- Some other suitable Christmas carol

We pray you, Lord, to purify our hearts
that they may be worthy to become your dwelling-place.
Let us never fail to find room for you,
but come abide in us,
that we also may abide in you,
for at this time you were born into the world for us,
and live and reign, King of kings and Lord of lords,
now and for ever.
William Temple (1881–1944)

Kindle, O Lord, in our hearts, we pray,
the flame of that love which never ceases,
that it may burn in us and give light to others.
May we shine for ever in your temple,
set on fire with that eternal light of yours
which puts to flight the darkness of this world;
in the name of Jesus Christ your Son our Lord.
Source unknown

Play or sing one of the following:
- I, the Lord of sea and sky *(332)*
- Holy, holy, holy *(286)*

May Christ the Light of the World,
scatter the darkness about us and before us.
May the bright light of Christ lead us
into the ways of peace and goodwill towards all.

EXPECT

Expect the Christ to seek room in your home and in your heart.
Make space every day for his coming to you. He will not force his
way in: invite him into your presence. Without this presence there
is an emptiness nothing can fill, not even Christmas feasting and
festivity. Expect to hear his call to your heart and give yourself
to him.

With Joseph and Mary, send out the crib and the infant Jesus
(see Week 1). Let them travel to as many houses as possible this
week. Sing or say 'Away in a manger' in each house they enter.
You may like to use this prayer:

Jesus Christ, you have come down
to lift us into the fullness of your kingdom.
You, dear Lord, have become human
that we may share in your divinity.
You have come to live among us
that we may be your friends.
We give you thanks for Christmas,
for the gift of your presence and yourself.

WEEK 6

Obeying and living

EXTRACT

Keep at least a minute of silence (in semi-darkness?)
Light five candles (or just one new one)

Pray

My dearest Lord,
be a bright flame before me,
be a guiding star above me,
be a smooth path beneath me,
be a kindly shepherd behind me,
today and for evermore.

St Columba (521-597)

Holy Jesus, Son of God,
as we long to hear the songs of the angels,
may we keep our eyes and hearts fixed on your coming.
As we travel with the shepherds to Bethlehem,
may we bow before your beauty and your majesty.
When we return to our homes, fill our days with your glory,
that we may rejoice in your love and abiding presence,
Jesus Christ, our Saviour and our God.

May the bright light of Christ enlighten our hearts,
shine in our minds and direct our journeying,
and scatter the darkness from the world.

Sing or listen to one of the following:
- While shepherds watched *(745)*
- Listen, let your heart keep seeking *(401)*
- Angels from the realms of glory *(36)*

EXCERPT

If possible, have two readers and leave a minute's gap between the readings.

Elijah on Sinai

Ahab told Jezebel all that Elijah had done, and how he had killed all the prophets with the sword. Then Jezebel sent a messenger to Elijah, saying, 'So may the gods do to me, and more also, if I do not make your life like the life of one of them by this time tomorrow.' Then he was afraid; he got up and fled for his life, and came to Beer-sheba, which belongs to Judah; he left his servant there.

But he himself went a day's journey into the wilderness, and came and sat down under a solitary broom tree. He asked that he might die: 'It is enough; now, O Lord, take away my life, for I am no better than my ancestors.' Then he lay down under the broom tree and fell asleep. Suddenly an angel touched him and said to him, 'Get up and eat.' He looked, and there at his head was a cake baked on hot stones, and a jar of water. He ate and drank, and lay down again. The angel of the Lord came a second time, touched him, and said, 'Get up and eat, otherwise the journey will be too much for you.' He got up, and ate and drank; then he went in the strength of that food forty days and forty nights to Horeb the mount of God. At that place he came to a cave, and spent the night there.

Then the word of the Lord came to him, saying, 'What are you doing here, Elijah?' He answered, 'I have been very zealous for the Lord, the God of hosts; for the Israelites have forsaken your covenant, thrown down your altars, and killed your prophets with the sword. I alone am left, and they are seeking my life, to take it away.'

He said, 'Go out and stand on the mountain before the Lord, for the Lord is about to pass by.' Now there was a great wind, so strong that it was splitting mountains and breaking rocks in pieces before the Lord, but the Lord was not in the wind; and after the wind an earthquake, but the Lord was not in the earthquake; and after the earthquake a fire, but the Lord was not in the fire; and after the fire a sound of sheer silence.

1 Kings 19:1-12

The shepherds and the angels

In those days a decree went out from Emperor Augustus that all the world should be registered. This was the first registration and was taken while Quirinius was governor of Syria. All went to their own towns to be registered. Joseph also went from the town of Nazareth in Galilee to Judea, to the city of David called Bethlehem, because he was descended from the house and family of David. He went to be registered with Mary, to whom he was engaged and who was expecting a child. While they were there, the time came for her to deliver her child. And she gave birth to her firstborn son and wrapped him in bands of cloth, and laid him in a manger, because there was no place for them in the inn.

In that region there were shepherds living in the fields, keeping watch over their flock by night. Then an angel of the Lord stood before them, and the glory of the Lord shone around them, and they were terrified. But the angel said to them, 'Do not be afraid; for see – I am bringing you good news of great joy for all the people: to you is born this day in the city of David a Saviour, who is the Messiah, the Lord. This will be a sign for you: you will find a child wrapped in bands of cloth and lying in a manger.' And suddenly there was with the angel a multitude of the heavenly host, praising God and saying,

'Glory to God in the highest heaven, and on earth peace among those whom he favours!'

When the angels had left them and gone into heaven, the shepherds said to one another, 'Let us go now to Bethlehem and see this thing that has taken place, which the Lord has made known to us.' So they went with haste and found Mary and Joseph, and the child lying in the manger. When they saw this, they made known what had been told them about this child; and all who heard it were amazed at what the shepherds told them. But Mary treasured all these words and pondered them in her heart. The shepherds returned, glorifying and praising God for all they had heard and seen, as it had been told them.

Luke 2:1-20

EXPAND

The story of Elijah shows the prophet depressed and despondent. He has faced much but now his own resources have run out. He has faced the opposition of 400 prophets, but cannot face one woman! We all know this situation; being human, our resources run dry. How do you cope then? Can you feel for Elijah and see yourself without energy and power? Have you learnt to rest? Sometimes we have to let go and let God! Feel yourself into the situation of Elijah in the wilderness and then on the mountain.

The shepherds were outside normal Jewish society. Dealing with sheep made them ritually unclean. They were outcasts on the fringe. Do you ever feel marginalised by society? Some people like to keep others on the edge of things. How do you feel in such a situation? Feel yourself into the situation of the shepherds on the hillside. You are working whilst others are sleeping or merrymaking. It can be a lonely, dangerous job. How do you feel being left in the dark? If a shepherd woke you to hear the angelic voices as they were fading away, how would you react?

EXPERIENCE

Do you see either of these stories speaking to your situation? Exhaustion and despair are common to all of humanity. The feeling of being rejected or kept on the edge is also common to us all. I like to explore the difference between breakdown in a life and breakthrough. Can you discover a time in your life that felt like a complete breakdown and in time proved a breakthrough to a richer and fuller life? Perhaps for some it is only when we have reached the feeling of being 'God-forsaken' that we discover he is always there.

EXPRESS

Can we really feel we are in need of a Saviour if we have never felt loss or dereliction? The dreadful comment on some people is that they have not lived enough to need the help and power of God, or so it seems. When we reach our lowest depths, do we know that 'underneath are the everlasting arms'? God does not send our exhaustion and rejection but he does work through it and in it. God never leaves us, not because we are worth it but because he loves us.

EXPOUND

When all is going well it is easy to feel that God is at work in your life, and is with you. It is far harder when life turns pear-shaped and nothing seems to be going well. We need to remember that God loves us whether we succeed or not. Elijah rejoiced in the power of God as he defeated the 400 false prophets of Baal. Elijah called down fire from heaven. At other times, he restored a dead boy to life, he stood against an evil king, and he even outran a chariot! Now when one woman was after him, he became depressed and despaired for his life. When Jezebel pursued him, Elijah said, 'It's too much, Lord.' He prayed, 'Take away my life. I might as well be dead.' Like anyone else, Elijah is a human being. In his exhaustion after his battle with the false prophets, he seeks to run from the next round of trouble. He felt as if God did not care. Remember all such feelings are liars. God always cares, never ceases to love us. God never sends us evil, though he may allow it to come. God's approach is 'Be of good cheer' or 'Fear not'. In Elijah's dereliction, God sustains him; he strengthens the prophet for the journey ahead. When God speaks to Elijah in the cave, he did not ask, 'What are you doing there?' He asked, 'What are you doing *here*?' God had not forsaken him; he was with Elijah throughout his journey. God would be with Elijah through the storm, the earthquake and the fire. In the stillness, at the mouth of the cave with his cloak wrapped about him, Elijah would hear God ask again, 'What are you doing here?' Though it was not where God wanted him to be, God was there with him. God had never left him. Elijah heard and obeyed the voice of God. It is not surprising that the Hebrew word used for hearing God implies obedience: to hear properly is to obey. Worship without obedience loses all meaning.

The shepherds' lot was not a happy one. They worked whilst others slept. Dealing with the sheep made them unclean and not fit for worship. They had to spend their nights looking to see if there was any danger to the flock; they were on the watch for robbers or wild beasts. This was no romantic situation but a dangerous one, and the work was often hard. The advantages were probably the silence and the need to be alert. It is interesting that St Patrick became far more aware of God when he was made to watch sheep on the hills of Ireland. Cuthbert's vision came when he was guarding sheep in the hills to the north of Lindisfarne. It is to the shepherds, 'the unclean outcasts', that the angel of God appears. I often wonder why the angel did not appear to someone in a synagogue and tell of the Messiah. Here grace is at work; these men did not deserve the visitation, they did not earn it. The appearance of the angel is about the grace of God, the unearned love that he offers to us. God gives of himself freely, what he asks of us is a response. Too often when God offers himself, he comes up against closed doors or hard hearts. 'No room at the inn' is a sign we often put up, excluding God from our lives and actions. The shepherds were receptive and open, so God could be revealed to them. Too often our own preconceived ideas and expectations do not allow our God to act.

The shepherds were disturbed by the glory of the Lord. Who were they that God should come to them? Who were they to be chosen? They were ordinary people, looking and watching; they were open to change. They were totally over-awed; they were afraid. 'Do not be afraid': wonderful words. I am told that 'Fear not' or 'Do not be afraid' appear 365 times in the Scriptures: one for each day of the year. The shepherds would be familiar with their Scriptures and would know such wonderful words as 'Do not be afraid. I have redeemed you, I have called you by your name, you are mine.' God in his grace and goodness calls each of us personally. He asks of us that personal response which is called faith. How wonderful to hear 'Glory to God in the highest heaven and peace on earth to those with whom he is well pleased.'

Once the vision fades, as it often does, its only test is action. Visions call for obedience or living out what we feel we have experienced. The shepherds left in the silence of the hills put the vision to the test and say, 'Let us go now to Bethlehem and see this thing that has happened, which the Lord has told us.'

What a strange sight it must have been, shepherds bowing down before the infant and telling Mary all that had happened. When the shepherds left, they went out singing praises to God for all that they had heard and seen. Too often we allow our vision to fade by not bringing God to mind in prayer and praise. The four Evangelists are known by name; with the shepherds we hear of the first evangelists, for they went out praising God for Christ come to earth.

EXULT

Give thanks that Jesus comes to you just as you are. He does not wait until you change: he does give you the opportunity for change and for newness of life.

Listen to:
- Hark, the herald angels sing *(266)*

> May the humility of the shepherds,
> the perseverance of the wise men,
> the joy of the angels,
> be God's gifts to us and to people everywhere
> this Christmas time.
> And may the blessing of the Christ-child
> be upon us always.
>
> *The Promise of His Glory*

Sing or listen to one of the following:
- Do not be afraid *(150)*
- O little town of Bethlehem *(508)*
- See him lying on a bed of straw *(589)*

EXPECT

Expect to meet God even when your feelings tell you that you are deserted. Remember feelings are often liars unless we teach them otherwise. Know that God comes to you; look for his glory in each day.

Send out the shepherds from the crib with a candle to represent the glory of God (see Week 1). Have on a card 'While shepherds watched' and also the following verse:

> What can I give him, poor as I am?
> If I were a shepherd I would bring a lamb.
> If I were a wise man I would do my part.
> Yet what I can I give him: give my heart.

Week 7
Living and sharing

EXTRACT

Keep at least a minute of silence (in semi-darkness?)
Light five candles (or just one new one)

Pray

Eternal light, shine in our hearts.
Eternal goodness, deliver us from evil.
Eternal power, be our support.
Eternal wisdom, scatter the darkness of our ignorance.
Eternal pity, have mercy upon us;
that with all our heart and mind and strength
we may seek your face and be brought by your infinite mercy
to your holy presence, through Jesus Christ our Lord. Amen.

Alcuin (735-804)

O God,
who by the leading of a star brought the wise men to Bethlehem,
guide us through each day and night on our journey of faith.
Lord, give us the courage to persevere,
that we are not put off in our search for you.
May we witness to your Gospel and rejoice in your glory.
May we seek to do your will until we enter the fullness of your
kingdom.
We ask this in the name of Jesus who came and lived among us.

May the bright light of Christ enlighten our hearts,
shine in our minds and direct our journeying,
and give light to the world

Sing or listen to one of the following:
- As with gladness men of old *(49)*
- We three kings of Orient are *(724)*
- Joy to the world *(370)*

EXCERPT

If possible, have two readers and leave a minute's gap between the readings.

The Valley of Dry Bones

The hand of the Lord came upon me, and he brought me out by the spirit of the Lord and set me down in the middle of a valley; it was full of bones. He led me all around them; there were very many lying in the valley, and they were very dry. He said to me, 'Mortal, can these bones live?' I answered, 'O Lord God, you know.' Then he said to me, 'Prophesy to these bones, and say to them: O dry bones, hear the word of the Lord. Thus says the Lord God to these bones: I will cause breath to enter you, and you shall live. I will lay sinews on you, and will cause flesh to come upon you, and cover you with skin, and put breath in you, and you shall live; and you shall know that I am the Lord.'

So I prophesied as I had been commanded; and as I prophesied, suddenly there was a noise, a rattling, and the bones came together, bone to its bone. I looked, and there were sinews on them, and flesh had come upon them, and skin had covered them; but there was no breath in them. Then he said to me, 'Prophesy to the breath, prophesy, mortal, and say to the breath: Thus says the Lord God: Come from the four winds, O breath, and breathe upon these slain, that they may live.' I prophesied as he commanded me, and the breath came into them, and they lived, and stood on their feet, a vast multitude.

Then he said to me, 'Mortal, these bones are the whole house of Israel. They say, "Our bones are dried up, and our hope is lost; we are cut off completely." Therefore prophesy, and say to them, Thus says the Lord God: I am going to open your graves, and bring you up from your graves, O my people; and I will bring you back to the land of Israel. And you shall know that I am the Lord, when I open your graves, and bring you up from your graves, O my people. I will put my spirit within you, and you shall live, and I will place you on your own soil; then you shall know that I, the Lord, have spoken and will act, says the Lord.'

Ezekiel 37:1-14

The visit of the wise men

In the time of King Herod, after Jesus was born in Bethlehem of Judea, wise men from the East came to Jerusalem, asking, 'Where is the child who has been born king of the Jews? For we observed his star at its rising, and have come to pay him homage.' When King Herod heard this, he was frightened, and all Jerusalem with him; and calling together all the chief priests and scribes of the people, he inquired of them where the Messiah was to be born. They told him, 'In Bethlehem of Judea; for so it has been written by the prophet:

And you, Bethlehem, in the land of Judah, are by no means least among the rulers of Judah; for from you shall come a ruler who is to shepherd my people Israel.'

Then Herod secretly called for the wise men and learned from them the exact time when the star had appeared. Then he sent them to Bethlehem, saying. 'Go and search diligently for the child; and when you have found him, bring me word so that I may also go and pay him homage.' When they had heard the king, they set out; and there, ahead of them, went the star that they had seen at its rising, until it stopped over the place where the child was. When they saw that the star had stopped, they were overwhelmed with joy. On entering the house, they saw the child with Mary his mother; and they knelt down and paid him homage. Then, opening their treasure chests, they offered him gifts of gold, frankincense, and myrrh. And having been warned in a dream not to return to Herod, they left for their own country by another road.

Matthew 2:1-12

EXPAND

There are times when we become totally wrung out, dried up with nothing else to give. Hope is in danger of being extinguished in our weariness. If something oppresses us for a long time it wears us down, and the feeling that God is not there creeps into our thoughts. This is the experience of many who have become prisoners of war or displaced persons. How would you react if you were born in captivity, or had endured it for about 40 years? If the people of Israel had lost sight of the Promised Land, they would have perished. In your own troubles, how do you keep faith and continue in hope? Put yourself in the position of Ezekiel trying to give hope to his people. How do you feel?

There are all sorts of captivities. There are work slaves, slaves to the system, people who have become captured by money or the need for popularity. Habits, fears, conventions all seek to ensnare us; our daily routine can make us captive. There are times when we need to move out, to follow the star. Can you find such situations in your life? How would you feel stepping into the unknown as one of the wise men did? Are we called to make the adventure of faith?

EXPERIENCE

Think about your own captivities: maybe you have created some of them yourself. Are you in the Valley of Dry Bones, or are you a pilgrim on the road to freedom? The collecting of wealth, the routine of worship without heart in gear, the fear of or the reality of illness can all seek to drain away our hopes. Can we say, 'Truly, Lord, our hope is only in you'?

EXPRESS

Do you see yourself in the Valley of Dry Bones? Are you prepared for the miracle of new life, new hope? The wise men were seekers, looking for a better life, looking for Jesus. Can you align yourself with one of the wise men and his gift?

EXPOUND

Ezekiel could not have been called by God at a more difficult time. The people he looked after were dispirited prisoners of war. They had been deported from their own land, losing homes, land and freedom. They had been in captivity a lifetime; some had died in captivity and others were born into it; many had forgotten what the freedom of their home land was like. They lacked enthusiasm, vitality: it was as if life had been drained out of them.

I once lived near Whitby, the home of the fictitious character Dracula. I was asked if I believed in Dracula who sucked life out of his victims! Of course I did not, but the story is popular because we all know what it is to awaken drained of life and without hope. Someone else asked me if I believe in life after death. Of course I do, but I also believe in life *before* death!

Ezekiel felt for his people who were saying, 'Our bones are dried up, our hope is gone: we are as good as dead.' He was brought by God to see the Valley of Dry Bones and asked, 'Can these dry bones live?' Impossible, if you think only on the human level. With God all things are possible; with the Spirit, the Lord of Life, there is hope for the driest of bones. He breathes new life into us as he did to the dry bones, as he did to the disciples in the

66

Upper Room. That which was broken is being restored. That which failed in its own might is revived by the power of God. What we saw as a breakdown, God sees as a breakthrough to new life. In his power God calls us to a fuller richer life in the Spirit.

Think over these words from D. H. Lawrence in his poem 'Shadows':

And if tonight my soul find her peace
in sleep, and sink into good oblivion,
and in the morning wake like a new opened flower
then I have been dipped again in god, and new created . . .
. . . And if in the changing phases of a man's life
I fall in sickness and in misery
my wrists seem broken and my heart seems dead
and my strength is gone and my life
is only the leavings of a life:
and still among it all, snatches of lovely oblivion and snatches
    of renewal,
odd wintry flowers upon the withered stem, yet new strange
    flowers
such as my life has not brought forth before, new blossoms of
    me.
Then I know that still
I am in the hands of the unknown god,
he is breaking me down to his oblivion
to send me forth on a new morning a new man.

The wise men were not all that wise. They went out not knowing where they were going; they even went to the wrong person by going to Herod. But they were men of faith and they followed the star. Some think they may have been astrologers. Not everyone who follows a star is an astrologer! Even if they were, they were looking for the Christ child and they came to him and offered him gifts. I know some who say they believe and stand far off.

The wise men were willing to move out, to leave all behind. They were not put off by threats of danger or by the mockery of others. They persevered until they came to where the Christ child was. Each of them had a personal need and something personal to offer. They would not stop until they came to the Christ child. It was with such an attitude that Augustine of Hippo wrote, 'Lord, our hearts are restless, until they rest in you.'

The gifts the wise men brought were full of symbolism. Gold, as always, stands for wealth and success. Gold is a sign of good times and of plenty; it is a symbol of power and the ability to buy what you want. Gold was seen as a symbol of prosperity and of God's favour. But gold cannot buy love! Gold cannot fill the human heart; it will make a good attempt but our hearts are bigger than all the gold in the world. The wise man knew this by experience and sought out the Christ child with all his heart.

Frankincense is a symbol of mystery and wonder. It was used in worship to signify a presence: it was a symbol of worship itself. This wise man knew what it was to come before mysteries and wonders. The mind delights in mysteries, but we as humans need more; we need a personal relationship. No amount of bowing before the mysterious will fulfil our greatest longing; we need to come before the personal God. Incense is a *sign* of the presence; it cannot replace it. This wise man found the presence of God in the Christ child and came before him with all his heart.

Myrrh is used as a painkiller. Pain can so often stop us from doing what we are capable of. Physical and mental pain hinders us and in this we need help. The heart also pains for love and for this there is no cure except love. Pain is hard to bear alone; so often the presence of a loving person relieves much of the pain. We cannot block off the pain that is an aching for God. If we sedate it, then our lives are sedated. The offering of myrrh was a sign that Jesus would share in our sufferings and 'by his wounds we are healed'. The wise man brought his pain and emptiness before the Christ child and came before him with all his heart.

More than their gifts, the wise men came and gave themselves to the Christ child. The gifts were symbols of their lives, but it was their lives they brought before him. They sought until they found. They shared a common journey in their search for meaning and for life in all its fullness. They saw visions and obeyed the call. They may have disappeared from history but we know their looking and their longings in our hearts. We also know that the Presence is more important than gifts.

EXULT

Give thanks that Jesus comes to you just as you are. He does not wait until you change: he does give you the opportunity for change and for newness of life.

I come before the Christ child,
I kneel before the infant,
I adore with the shepherds,
I worship with the wise men,
I love him with Mary and Joseph,
I wonder at the 'Word made flesh',
I bow before the mystery.
I sing glory to God with the angels.
I will travel this day rejoicing,
glorifying and praising God.

Sing or listen to one of the following:

- What child is this (729)
- Hard, the glad sound (265)
- Go, tell it on the mountain (243)

EXPECT

Expect to hear the call of God in the longings of your heart. Rejoice that he travels with you on life's journey and seeks to know you.

Send out the wise men from the crib set (see Week 1). With the wise men send out the carol 'We three kings from Orient are' and also the following words:

What can I give him, poor as I am?
If I were a shepherd I would bring a lamb.
If I were a wise man I would do my part.
Yet what I can I give him: give my heart.

A candle can represent the leading of the star, a light in our darkness, the Presence of Christ.

The group may like to use this act of praise at the end of the sessions:

For the God who seeks us when we hide,
give thanks and praise.
For the God who finds us when we seek,
give thanks and praise.
For Moses bowing before the mystery of God,
give thanks and praise.
For the disciples awaking on the mountain,
give thanks and praise.
For Isaiah's awareness that God is on his throne,
give thanks and praise.
For the obedience and Christ-bearing of Mary,
give thanks and praise.
For the sustaining and renewing of Elijah,
give thanks and praise.
For the angel's song to the shepherds,
give thanks and praise.
For Ezekiel and new life to dry bones,
give thanks and praise.
For the journeying and offering of the wise men,
give thanks and praise.
For the coming of God into the world,
give thanks and praise.
For his presence with us now,
give thanks and praise.